MW01248721

UMBERTO'S NIGHT

UMBERTO'S NIGHT

Kathleen Hellen

Washington Writers' Publishing House
Washington, D.C.

COVER ART by Rosemary Liss

COVER DESIGN by Drew Brezinski

TYPESETTING by Barbara Shaw

LIBRARY OF CONGRESS CATALOGUING-IN-PUBLICATION DATA

Hellen, Kathleen.

    Umberto's night / Kathleen Hellen.

       p. cm.

    ISBN 978-0-931846-99-1 (pbk. : alk. paper)

    I. Title.

    PS3608.E39225U63 2012

    811'.6–dc23

2012023885

Printed in the United States of America

WASHINGTON WRITERS' PUBLISHING HOUSE
P. O. Box 15271
Washington, D.C. 20003

Sid

To one of my favorite
mentors and colleagues —
a fellow in the art of poetry,
a true craftsman and son
of the muses.

Much love
Kathleen

— FOR MY SONS DAVID AND ZACHARY

AND FOR ETSUKO AND JOE, MY PARENTS
ON THE WHITE ROAD AHEAD

GRATEFUL ACKNOWLEDGMENTS to the editors of the following publications in which these poems first appeared, sometimes in earlier versions:

"Lift Her to the Witnesses" in *The 5-2: Crime Poetry Weekly*; "Notches" in *Appalachian Heritage*; "Smoke" in *Barrow Street*; "Why I Weep for Six White Handkerchiefs" in *Beltway Poetry Quarterly*; "Slag" in *Blue Collar Review*; "Abducted from the Keats" in *The Broome Review*; "Sleep of Stones" in *Cave Wall*; "Palpable" in *The Chesapeake Reader*; "What the Body Knows" in *Confluence*; "From the Metro" and "Goodnight, Irene" in *Connotation Press*; "Ghostwalk" in *The Cortland Review*; "Oh, Cisco" in *The Dos Passos Review*; "Waste of Culture Waste of State" in *Evergreen Review*; "How Light Bends at the Exxon" in *Gargoyle Magazine*; "Diamond Life" in *Harpur Palate*; "The Summer We Were Hungry" in the *H.O.W. Journal*; "Approximate Wall" in *In Our Own Words*; "Fifty Gypsies Come With Care Instructions" in *In Posse Review*; "Fear, Desire— Feathers That Fly" in *The Innisfree Poetry Journal*; "Stay" in the *James Dickey Review*; "Wondrous Pitiful" in *J Journal*; "Last Weekend Before Winter" in *Kestrel*; "The Persistence of Memory" in *Lake Effect*; "Nine Circles" in *Little Patuxent Review*; "Che Guevara's Fingers" in *MAYDAY Magazine*; "Clackers" in *Mead*; "As Myself" in *The Merton Seasonal*; "Three Views of the Mon" in *Now & Then*; "The Fire Sermon: Follansbee Coke Plant" in *Painted Bride Quarterly*; "He Opens Doors, He Closes Them" and "Neither Shall You Steal" in *Pank*; "Anthem at Graduation" in *Passager*; "Once, in a Yellow Wood" in *Poemeleon*; "The Homecoming" in *Poetry Northwest*; "A Congress of Monsters" in *The Potomac*; "Ritual of Little Heads" in *RUNES*; "Naming" in *Sakura Review*; "Hobo Jungle" in the *Seattle Review*; "Aubade" and "The Great Tortoise of Ray's Sports Tavern" in *Superstition Review*; "Dear Dust" in *Swink*; "Friendly Borders" in *Terrain.org*; "Eight" in the *Urbanite*; "Belly Song" and "Seasonal" in *Yellow Medicine Review*.

My gratitude, as well, to Brandel France de Bravo, Sid Gold, Dan Gutstein, Holly Karapetkova, and Patric Pepper for their untiring support of this book; to Rosemary Liss and Drew Brezinski for their abundant talents; and to Barbara Shaw for her scrupulous attention to detail. And for their discernment, their generosity, I thank E. Ethelbert Miller, Richard Peabody, Kim Roberts, and Rhett Iseman Trull.

"... as if along a river, you go by an invaded city which is being sacked, with the rape of the women, theft of jewels, torture of the mayor; the city burns like a match, drunken pirates sprawled on piles of kegs sing obscene songs; some, completely out of their heads, shoot at the visitors; the scene degenerates, everything collapses in flames ...."

—*Travels in Hyperreality*, Umberto Eco

Contents

1

As Myself

From room to room she looked, found me, found the lamp,
swept the shards up in a pan, shook her head —
(She must have felt it in her bones when Daddy got the strap.)

lied, said the thing I did she did,
said she broke the lamp,
said she'd pay in wages
every day a little bit.

Never saw her after that,
never heard again her sing
the chariots so low.
Looked when I was grown
into alleys between Fayette, 25th,
into projects like the photos of Soweto.

Found clockers on the block. The crack-lit cornered.
The ashy asking anything to spare.
They sleep in boxes, eating air.
They break and enter. They don't repair.

Found mothers in the stations of despair.
The takers taking theirs from copped Sowebo.

Never had the chance to ask
forgiveness for myself,
for everyone, still asking,
every day a little bit.

Oh, Cisco

I wore the miniskirt they made me wear. Filled
ketchup bottles. Six of them on leave from the Queen Mary said,
"Hey, make for us a dozen of those milkshakes," and I quit.
Too much heart for all that shit.
On the black-and-white tv for twenty-five a week with rabbit
ears, the Cisco Kid reran his film career.
"Oh, Pancho!" they joked. We toked a little weed,
coaxed into the jelly jar cockroaches the size of fucking Twinkies.
I cut my hair to eight-tracks of Santana. Seconal and beer.
Billie started needles and we split.
I got a job working nights at a peep show on the pier.
He called me up. "Angel," he said. "Angel, you got to come. I'm sick."
His hands shook like Jell-O when I did. "Let's went," I said.
"Texas. Arizona. Nuevo Mexico," the "x" pronounced like "h,"
like Cisco Kid. "Anywhere but here."
He closed his eyes and horses spurred into the
iridescence, reared.

Why I Weep for Six White Handkerchiefs

I took it for a sign. A message in a bottle traveling seas
of African mahogany consigned to me. The slavery
of forms. Decades from the master craft of 1963.
This dresser. This survivor.
A noble joining. A handsome carpentry
I lavished with a lemon-scented sheen.
I rubbed. I worked the detail, pulled the drawers.
A trust of headlines lined the war:
"Top Russ pianist and wife defect."
"Three towns in Laos fall to Communists."
These oddities:
— Stockings (*coffee bean*)
— A letter posted Washington, D.C.,
        in faded print predicting,
          "Dear Comrade, you have been elected...."
— Photos of a girl with good hair dressed in pink
— A pack of six white handkerchiefs.
A second hand of histories. The grief of each.
Russian or Laotian. Vietnamese. African-
      American.
      Never finished.

Intake

Cinderblock walls
with "Please God Help Me" scrawled.
The sweltry cell mimics flesh.

Someone's scared her daughter won't get
picked up after school. Another's puked.
The blonde who's been reduced
to boosting Kraft as cheese tells you, please,
don't lose it,

or they'll strip you,
put you in a room
all by yourself.

You wait your turn to call.
You wait your turn to soot the card with prints.
Best case, you'll get probation.

"They were nice to you," a guard says,
distressed your hands are cuffed in front
instead of twisted at your back.
You remember the arrest.
He let you get out of the van to stretch your legs.

As gently as a lover,
he brushed the hair from your face.

Nine Circles

The boy heard
ringing in his ears

that left a hole
in her thigh
the size
of a button.

It bled in her hand,
into the patterned sofa he hid under,
and he ran,

feet locomoting
like the Road Runner from Coyote.
River Street retreated

into bars and liquor stores.
He must have turned the block
nine times or more

before
Miss Geneva called him in
her tiny kitchen,
gave him lemonade, said,
"Don't be afraid, Jabo.
Your momma and your daddy
just don't see things quite the same."

The Homecoming

Beyond the C Lot where I'd parked and Druid Park,
I thought it was a dog

until the light revealed a shape the light delayed.
Dark Runner
between this world and the other.
He came to say he'd passed the last exam —
Greenmount, North, West Belvedere.
The streets he'd pledged. Fraternities of
blood he had attempted to essay in fifty minutes.
Acolytes of signs. The violence of colors.
Of dangerous teachers. How could I compare?
All I had were outlines. Study guides.

They knew his name. They'd sprayed it on a wall tattooed
and facing west. A deadly roster counting fists.
Despite a diagnostic promising the "A,"
the ledger of his grades, the last accounting showed
only empty cells, the empty spaces.
Quizzes, papers where I'd added up the
zeroes since October. He'd missed
so many classes when his brother
in a suit appeared to say,
"He's dead. He won't be back."

Now the board's erased. The lesson booked or
bagged or dumped into a trunk on Cedarcroft.
Rims spinning.

Anthem at Graduation: The HBCU

For James Weldon Johnson (1871-1938) and Jimi Hendrix (1942-1970)

We sing the Book of Numbers.
Mums, gladiolas swelling in their ribboned dress.

Vaudeville of rejoicing, each a Lazarus.
A choir of black faces staged.

Not run away but faith rehearsed
in normal schools for coloreds,
in run-down auditoriums.

There is a prayer after despair.
Be not afraid.

Aubade

i.

Light leans in. I watch you leave. A black man traveled over,
melting into slush that melts to nothing much.
First man who'd been to prison, back,
I ever asked to bed. First dazzling.
"A novelty," you said, chopping slabs
out of the ice. The snow dismissing color.

ii.

The white boys you remember shouted "nigger" as you fled.
Your lead leg over meters, as if practicing for track.
You said you lost your cap as you ran, turned the corner.

iii.

Chocolates (*dark as you*) as the amenities. To fit the people we might be,
they'd hung robes as white as sheets on the adjoining door. The same
civilities as in the store in Fredericksburg we toured. Battle maps.
Confederate flags as flanked reminders
of another, darker war. Darker yet,
not anecdote: A fact: A woman with a mop,
struck to see us kissing on the stairs going up.
Witness to the sheets.

iv.

In this town too old for beginnings: "House For Sale."
The same ochre tint on stately sandstone chiseled
on the wall of Trenton's prison. You stepped away
to get perspective on the newly painted shutters.
Hinted we see others. Said you never plan
the way a free man plans. Instead, we talked about
the weather as we walked uphill in drizzle
to the Jefferson Hotel.

v.

Half a cigarette to get you to the exit. Ahead, more snow.
I know no name for it in Greek, though
it is the closest I have come, the closest I have been:
Sex as liberation. Dance as feeling.
You taught me: Swerve to stop. Look behind
where I am heading. Sing.

Eight

Some murders surface off the tourist
promenade. They float like strange *velella*
in the Giant jellies' bloat,
where rock fish tangle up
with cigarette butts, with mothers' sons
in six degrees of syphilis, HIV.

who got shot in Druid Park?
whose throat was cut?

North Avenue and Longwood, the hearses double park.
Mourners mute as pit bulls with their throats slit, shut.
Outlines of a city's fate in chalk.
Balloons and flowers
now, where hot dogs boiled
summer nights the deals went south,
where they lit the Dawsons' house. Killed seven.

No witnesses protected. No belief
in signs that read: "Believe."
In what, the darrells ask? Drive-bys
in the choke. Slums spun into gold for
other folk. The dead who raise themselves.

No More Killer Than We All Are — Triggered

He scores in dark halls of assault. Impersonates the weapon
on nights the cruiser clocks its revolutions. 100 mph
on every MLK that runs through every project.

"I popped him," says the cop. Tail lights on the pimped Mercedes
shattered. Velocities of force to entertain the rats that havoc sewers.
"Bad sign," he says, when bean pie and the bow ties hawk

the Second Coming. Even Chinese takeout's boarded up.
"What's another punk selling junk to six-year-olds?"

2

He Opens Doors, He Closes Them

Ladies first, they always said. He feels like he's in high school. The boys surrendered chairs. They paid for dates. A white agenda. There was a popular cologne by Fabergé in green-glass bottles. Football games. A dry champagne for weddings and anointments of the king. The patriarch of rich plantations. He watches as she sips her lemonade, as if she graced a white veranda. No doubt his swagger is a cop, is criminal. His finger triggers on the winning like the spoils he has driven. To capture or embrace the narrow of her waist. Defend her honor. A patriot. A player. Will she surrender? The single operation of his arm commands her gender.

Che Guevara's Fingers

He knows about the CIA. Bolivia. Her Coke is sweating.
She saw the movie: Guevara in that black beret
in the days before the army had him cornered.
"They gave him up for maize," he says. Laughs.
Sizes up the guests at nearby tables.

How did they connect on the Internet?
What whispers answered to occasion?
Did she think he could wrap her
in the jacket of his ways?
Save her

from trails in wooded parks,
bus stops, dim-lit garages, the streets
where globes illuminate a cultivated terror?

He pays the check. Enables.
"How do you know
the man you kill
is the man
you're supposed to kill?"
He wiggles his fingers.

Friendly Borders

Foreign to me how she looks in exile
from herself — bottle blond and bruised.
The trill of "Carlos, Carlos" drilled
into my dreaming. I stop my ears to trespass
of these row-house walls. The throated moans
deported like a raft of drained Coronas
to the fence I'd staked with flags
and pinwheel daisies —
just to keep the field rats out.
The *cholo* squirrels.
The rabbits breeding more
than rabbits can afford.

Fifty Gypsies Come With Care Instructions

First, the stem —
cut slantwise through the vein.
Thorn and petal guards remove, then
powders to dissolve into a bluing
drunk from bottom until leaves detach.
A vase. Arrange for showing. Display
for succor when occasions are the same.
The same hint of blight
in tubes as green as envy me
the music that we danced to.
We give as we are used.
The second cut is harder.

Wondrous Pitiful

She swore, i' faith ...'Twas pitiful,
'twas wondrous pitiful. — Othello

His rough vocabulary
enlarged her sense of sorrow.
His language — carnal — conjured
cannibals in Trenton, Rahway.
If he hadn't skipped the chow line,
he might have died, he told her.
A shank. A screwdriver.
A life in hostage for a smoke.
He said they'd cut a throat so deep
the head lay back between the shoulders.
Men like dogs in capture pissed themselves.
She listened at his feet. Oh, the wondrous
world he mapped in her pale imagination.
She kissed his scars, lived his skin. Puissant. Vital.
The witchcraft that he spoke was practiced, anecdotal.
He put his hand around her throat — after that,
nothing could distract her.

Evidentiary

He's here in the bones of her throat,

in the pews of a hearing room,
even if she doesn't turn around to look.
Her plea is a piercing

in district court — what he might do,
when he'll do it. The judge who hears
the case has heard it all.
A roll call of injunctions —
Johnson. Abdulilla. Jenerette —

before the evidence presents
a bludgeoning as murder.
Proof,
duly noted.

He's here in a green polo shirt,
even if his lawyer wears a suit.

One by one the summoned
stand in their exclusions.
"Is anyone in your family a member of the police?"
"Is anyone in your family a victim?"
Johnson. Abdulilla. Jenerette.

He Closes In

He wears the coat of brother uncle dad.
She probably knows him.

The scene, a factory street in summer.
Zooming in: A junkyard where he's hunched.
The universal logic of his musk. The myth rewritten as
No Swan Becoming. A Clockwork Something.
Or: Bookmark

in her throat, the moth in pupa
as instruction. His knack for dungeons in
The Silence of the Lambs.

His fingers stitch the telling out of skin —
the shredded petal-tissue of her sex.
The pansies in her grip.
The wrecked susans.

Abducted from the Keats

He left her without breasts,
stripped her like a tree like Ovid's laurel,
dumped her in a lake in a desert in a ditch.

A swan. A trope. An open book.
A virgin with their meters blank as bone
shoved down her throat.

Take Marie. Thirteen.
A boneyard of her kind at the border.

Take Saramba. Four.
Weaponed in the war.
A tribe's retaliation.

First Night, First Right.
First of many wives in Salt Lake City.

Here's what I'm given:
No point throwing stones
at glass that always breaks.
Forgive infatuation.
Forgive the saints
who drink you from a skull cup, then repent
come Lent — kings
who feed you pearls in tales of take.

Serial or strangler? *What men or gods are these?*

Lift Her to the Witnesses

Lay her flat.
Open airways, pinch the nose and
every three or four (*which is it?*)

seconds, breathe, breathe
the failed resuscitation.

Her lips beget the bluing. Lying on her back.
The rattling from her purse-d lips like snoring
isn't sleeping. Is she breathing? we ask,
standing by the "Help me!"
Then collapsed.

Ghostwalk

Tide Point in the bay.
The ducks aloft, gliding in the shimmer.
A mother and her chicks. A wind
picks up slightly as the water taxi launches
its last blow: One long leaving.

Ports in Little Italy, the Fort.
Lighter than the wind, the ghosts cavort.
Captains, shanghaied boys. Sweethearts
in their corsets or tattooed
like these young lovers kissing in the shadows
at the pier, holding on to
phantoms of each other, drunk on beer.

Visitors to open air,
to streetlights quickening along the planks.
Witnesses to tall ships,
tankers, houseboats in the slip.

A world on the verge
of some distress.
A woman, for example, on the tipsy edge,
leaves the bar, casts off
on cobbled streets. Inside herself,
the compass. Did he mean it
when he said he'd take her in the dinghy?
If she had to, could she swim?

One foot out,
the other, out where night is anchored —
short/long/short/long.
Out where night is vast, heaving.

Palpable

2 a.m. aromas
lead in warm degrees
to Ann Street's sugared yeast.
The night rolls up its sleeves.
Two in dusty aprons ease
pans from blackened ovens.

Incandescent in the window,
the kiwi's cut like jade,
the berries float in glaze —

fruit more real
than any fruit we've eaten.

We breathe our fog. Write love
backward on the glass. Blow
kisses through our giggles.

Where we've parked a long way off —
a drunkard's quilt. A riddle.

3

Seasonal

Enough, I said. Then::

A surge, a breach in the startled plywood.
An army impeached. The bodies in sheets.
Quarantines. The tunnel to managed quarters.

The summer that followed was heat.
The media in helicopters thinly thoraxed.
Then::

Birds in both ears disappeared.
Only the attitude — rain.
A room without doors. A wailing
within. People like rain.
                    An ice flow of feeling that lengthened
as days
in the solstice
shortened.
Then:

Zoloft. Remote.
I couldn't sleep.
I taped all the *Nature* shows scripted.
I turned down my children in sleep.
I cried in the manner of sleeves.

I scrolled through the cancellations.
No school today. Activities delayed.
No dogs but strays.
No squirrels on the roof where I signaled.

Into winter and spring, no fractals emerging.
Then::

Faint lung of pink. A petal unpurling.
Then::

Grass. A kernel of yellow
things I forgot.

The Imaginarium of Attractions

        Enter —
centuries confused. The ruse of weavers,
masons buttering brick. Replicas of forge,
stabled horses. Trick

of hammers. Hemp and licorice.
Apex of the This-
Inside-A-This.

What of your hand inside my hand?
A kiss? A restaurant and a foil swan
delivered by the chef — *voila!*

Reenactments of the past
without the past. Memories
of what we never had
more like beliefs.
        Leave —

what seems a cast. Living holographs.
The night inside a night until
attention must be tipped
        to darkness in its layers.

From the Metro

We are skimming landscapes, a lap of magazines. The city quitting
under hunched shoulders, its streets implied by signs, the grid.
Bare trees hide nothing. Detritus of foam and fuel and wrappers.
Shrouds of plastic in the cables. Carcasses of steel.
We are going nowhere. Traffic fences flight. The right of exit
lost to left of reason. We tour the last occasion of the rain.
A forest dreaming winter. I press my hand to where a
sparrow might have crashed into what had seemed transparence.
Doors are suddenly flung open — a rush.
I do not recognize my own reflection.

The Persistence of Memory

An open space was where a window used to be on the fifth floor of
the dorm. Fifty feet below, on top of the glass, a young man lay face
down in the snow. The first on the scene, I leaned in. "Hang on,"
I whispered. As the siren approached, I looked for a gash. A cut.
A bone wrenched sideways, crushed. Despite the cold, my face was
flushed. I measured distance to ground, the force of impact. I slipped
off my coat, laid it over his shoulders, as onlookers gathering asked:
"What happened? How?" Then medics pushed me back. That night on
the news they called it a prank he had staged when his girlfriend left
him. Something like: "Jilted lover fakes suicide attempt." I remembered
then the glass — a perfect pallet in the snow. Nothing was smashed.
Nothing was broken. Images persisted as I washed the dishes. Had he
heard what I whispered? I suffered in my thoughts a hundred injuries,
then a dish slipped from my hand. Shattered.

Listing
— U-1105

We grope toward floodlights,
shot line hooked. The relic sunk

in brackish water off the coast
of the Potomac. Dark
salvage.

Experiment of war
we anchor for,
as sea rolls out its catch.

Evidence to wreck
the surface of our knowing.

What crimes we soon forget,
strapping tanks,
pitching backward
to archive the recent damage
to the hatch —

the savage hull
blasted open —

as minnows school in certainties
so small

they vanish in the caps.

Sound Bites

Something manic in the stepped-up ceaseless effort.
The smoke released in contrails. A muscled scouring
as black hawks dredge a hard line's civil strife.
A sticking point in Palestine. The sky's rebuke.

A man who's tired of it all reloading.
The rat-tat-tat-tat as barricade. As natural.
He looks into the camera. A second's delay.
"I'm sorry," the reporter says,
slipping dangerously close to

engagement. A man over there,
in Arabic, simplifying: "They shoot at legs to stop us."
All of them crying. The kids soaking wet.
The dishes. The mess. A man with a gun.
His wife on the stained linoleum.
"It's over," he says.

Harborplace Hotel

Silence is the key she swipes to access.

HBO. Internet access. A skyline she never imagined.
A harbor she almost believes.

She speaks the language of passport.
Of guests who pillow on chocolates,
wrapped in the gold of the Aztecs.
"Do Not Disturb," the sign says.

Silence is the argument.

A bed to make, a wage.
She washes sheets
for kings, for queens —
the sheets turned down at the borders.

What makes the difference but action?

Dear Dust

There's a light where you gathered,
though in grade school I hardly knew you.

You sat in the back,
your head in the recitations.
Chariot races. The shield and gun.
Sputnik. The Soviet threat.

Campaigns you embraced, though they warred
long before you were born.
Your desk like a helmet,
you did as a soldier,
as you were told.

Duty to fathers. To arms in the underworld.

After high school you didn't come back. Light
without heat. The color shoved off. Dust
in a land of caesars.

The mud of My Lai became you, dressed
in the garlands of doubt.

Approximate Wall

Rubbings

1.

On a lawn chair with a Coke, he plots
trajectories. Villages he never sees
until the smoke lifts,
the jungle disappears in urgent orange.

In December, he flies home.
His sin: he couldn't win.
He dreams of offshore gun boats aimed
at darkness.

Snow is lightly falling
in Charleston, West Virginia.
He shivers in his summer whites,
a captain's uniform.

2.

Bunkered at the Waffle House,
the war without relief
relived in cigarettes.

He can't forget:
The slant-eyed girl
who blacked his boots for tips.
Still, he'd take her home with him,
but there's a husband, so he thinks.
Others, thousands like them, him —

working sleeping hungry weeping
scared shitless.

Funny, how his hand shakes,
how the match exacts resemblance.
A pack of smokes like ammo.

3.
He separates the dead from those he knows
are dying.
Counts tags, body bags.
Counts the days until he's shipped back
to the States: Two hundred fifty-five.

His mind divides. Triage
of the crimes.
Jungled in his eyes,
the fear trap sprung.

A tyger
in the syndrome
on a rooftop in D.C.
The yakety-yak trajectory
sneaking through the trees.
The crosshairs of the moon.

He separates the dead from those he knows
don't count.
Tags, body bags.
He could crush her with his mouth.

Clackers

September takes your order. Bowls of glistening aphrodisiac
in red or milky chowder. A dozen shooters shucked.
We'd like to wear a necklace made of mantle.
Pearls of Venus smooth as alabaster.
The world's the oyster.

October's raw. The grass bed's thin. The spawning stock's declining.
The tv's treading sand in Humvees in Iraq. *Our legs like seaweed*
tangle. Our song a siren's laughter. Ten legs navigate Wellbutrin.

November's tapped. The harbor where we wandered was a bar
where jellies float, where fishing boats drop anchor.
With tentacle and fin. With cannibals.
What solid things to cling to when the tide comes in?

December and the college girls are gone.
We drink another beer. Another shell-shocked year.
How to haul us up?

Belly Song

I sit in the front row of
bleachers — cheap seats for greater grief.
My son,

the tribe in his ribs,
the strength in him keen, huddled,
runs through the hits, breathes
through the pale ghost of stitches
these games that go long into hard victories.

Who knows how long we have them?
When sirens call to streets,
when one sends back his fatigue,

another's enlisted.

The bones of an open Humvee. The bones
at a roadside checkpoint.

It might be that we swallow them:
A belly song. A flag sent home.
A rosary like dog tags.

A triage of crows flies over.
My son

packs up his cleats.
The fog of his breathing surrenders.
He limps to the car where I tender
his wounds. The bones
of a cradle breaking.

Stay

She's gone when he gets there,
when he hikes the wounded trail, north or south
depending on the compass of his hunger.
Follows John Deere cap and flannel through the
blackest Appalachians. Duct tape on the
running rehabbed van. Miles of meadow farm
and shoulder where he camps. Stay, he begged her.
Hummed her chummy song. Treated her as if
she were a wild bird at the feeder.
Trajectories of ambush and surrender
like in Nam. No one had a weapon.
Nothing had exploded when he ran.
Glory or dumb luck. He thought he might have
won, but like the apple scent of
summer she is gone.

4

Three Views of the Mon

1. woman

Smoke, soot, sulfur, stink —
how did she come to this place but falling?

He made her laugh,
despite the knack for sorrow
in this barren slag.

She dreams the poisoned river.
It calls to her, milk weary as she warms the bottle at the stove,
puts the cat out for the night, bolts the door.

Headlights cross the ceiling. The pulled chain ticks
on the bulb like a burned-out star.

2. warrior

"Money go to hell-a" is the joke he tells.
Two Indians on a boat ... wampum in the whelk
that sink to bottom.

He finishes a beer before the bar clears out.
The graveyard shift clocks in
the No-Way-Out

but what Montana did,
Namath.

Not everybody can. Not every Joe is cruising
in a brand-new Dodge, high rolling.

Not everybody wants it bad
enough.

The river sizzles
like a steak with every quench
going down.

3. Monongahela

The river migrates toward its gravities.

The blackest seam along its bank a vein to tap
and tar until the soft addiction opens
like a sore. The barges chugging ore

to volatilities up north, to Monessen,
to orange rock and eyesore, to Homestead.

Tonight the sky ignites. A frankenstein
of furnaces. The weird Northern Lights,
borealis of the coking.

White steel like water pouring.

The Fire Sermon: Follansbee Coke Plant

A rotten egg is cracked against the sky.
Nothing
       you can see beyond the scrim
of smoke, the glow of furnaces,
               the choke.

Can't tell the chug of the machinery
from barges pushing in another load
of coke.

       No delight in things tonight:
The swimming pool, the motor boat, the camper
hitched out back.
            No relief.
Not even in the shallow water lapping
at the edge of some belief.

The river sweats its tar into baptism.
Listen. Dead branches in the current shift.

Feel the catfish breathe. Feel
the waves ascend.

Layoff at No. 9

He brokers failure:
"I'm retired now."
"I know,"

I say, and let him go on with the kinfolk:
"Delphine had the baby up." A thing or two about it.

The easy chatter
wafting through the clatter of the tables bussed.
The Way-You-Like-It Eggs.
The waitresses with fresh-brewed pots for things discussed
at Shoney's. A woodpile left to puddles.

Only the chain-link between us
like dogs snapping air.

Slag

Did we think the red horizon was too beautiful?
Marked its brilliance as forgiveness?

Pale waste of it, trucked off and dumped into the mountains of refuse
like mountains of the moon where nothing grew.
A cratered landscape dimming.
What of stink? The lethal plume?
The sulfurous river running from the furnaces that loomed?
The metals we set free?

We married steel-toe boots,
loved the sirens that seduced us,
the change of shift that wooed us
to drowning in the gases chugged like beers.

What fills us up when lungs collapse? What face stares back
in skin like rash, discolored from the heat?

Who moves inside the legs that drag?
The back, a broken shovel.

The Summer We Were Hungry

After rain, she digs out with a spatula
the dappled milk — our fill
of fawn-gilled, cream,

browning in a skillet —
the spores our bellies quarrel over. Butter,
salt. If there is some

or we do without. True morel or failure
is a Chinese hat.
A coma. The harvest

ghost of moon might bring her back
as noses press to glass inside
the deadly Pontiac. We are fast,

already sleeping. Goat's head —
if she finds it — fries like steak.

A Pillar of Fire by Night

There's a deck where the wind plays cards.
A row house for sale next to four more for sale
on the same street, in the same city,

absent people. The mattresses in exodus stack up.
A bike with pink handles. A few solid chairs.
Street signs lead to banishment in skyline.
Default's stiff arms, like armed guards like
whitewashed seraphim brandishing swords.

Only the memory
of purposes concealed. Of offices
tight lipped in their failures, dark.
A world was there, then it wasn't.

Used to be a mower knew the edges of the season.
The street was swept, the snow in catacombs dug out
for access in the rare evacuation. Used to be
the summer strung its lanterns in the backyard
of a birth. A graduation. Charcoal and the joss
of rib sauce rising: Offerings to gods.

If the lawn chairs part, if we make it,
surely there are summers of our innocence at hand.
Surely there are funnel cakes and sugar spun into
transfiguration.
                Come back, Moses.
Bring the Ring of Tongues. The tattooed girl in braids
resembles Mary. The kid who flips a skateboard, water walks.

Bring the drunks in hi tops dancing. Bring the cops.
The thugs. The vets in powered wheelchairs.

Bring the Sacred Heart, all judgment cordoned off.
We are lost in wilderness, in wandering.

The Great Tortoise of Ray's Sports Tavern

Summer meant us to be kind, so we fed it red skin
peanuts as if it were a squirrel.
Then someone said, "They don't eat peanuts."
We didn't know. It seemed to us a stone
in a pond they'd drained and painted blue
to confuse it. The boys from St. Luke's cut
with far-flung sticks their initials in its shell.
The sticks piled up, the leaves. A mountain's
weight of season on its back before the season
put its boot inside the door at Ray's Sports Tavern.
We didn't see it anymore until Donora's championship.
A trophy nailed to Ray's hinged door.
A bowl unhinged of its exquisite soup.

Hobo Jungle

Beans, fists of green tomatoes –
his blessing on her house was seed.

When the garden fell to weed,
he lugged coal to feed her stove, fastened hinges.

When the garden fell to weed,
he shouldered kit and jug and tramped down tracks
to where the campfires built from railroad ties and
driftwood burned like signals in the darkness.

Reruns of *Lassie*

It was a tv place called Calverton. No place at all.
No lakeshore with the greenery I believed
were trees when U.S. Steel shut down.
The "world's largest nail mill,"
the sign atop the factory gate announced
before it closed. No work for worth. No fin-tailed cars.
No chance of Timmy asking: "What is it, Lassie?
Who needs help?" No dog at all. Or gone.
Devoured by wolves. The dogs with bigger teeth.
We heard the stories. They stood in line
for day-old bread. For soup ladled thin. Later,
when I got older, I found out episodes were filmed
on Holden Ranch in California;
the Franklin Canyon Reservoir in Santa Monica;
Williamsburg, Virginia; New Orleans; the Braille trail
in the San Bernardino National Forest;
the Columbia Gorge Log Flume.

No place at all, as credits roll, the theme song plays,
as Lassie, bandaged, limps into the woods.
No one asks: Who was master?

Last Weekend Before Winter

Last night a bear was close. The deer upwind.
He asks which trees are those so brilliant

yellow. Oak, the poplar? Pale-blue lichen paint
the bark he used to mark when he was young.
A boy in Virginia. Milkweed leans with pods.
The monarch hides in chrysalis.

From pop-up tents beside the glass recycling
bins, a radio relives the times he
danced to The Watusi. He might have said
the stars were dim — she was the lens
through which he saw things clearly.
Since she'd been gone
he hid the absence of her hands with fists
stuffed in his pockets. Cap pulled down,

eyes unseeing all the stars, the pulsing.
Stuck inside the wandering, he might have said
the trail was getting harder, the hot dogs
not as good. He slivered moons, he worried woods.

Naming

Gettysburg at dusk

At Little Round Top all the crops are gone.
The ghosts of houses looted, the stores of
corn stolen from the cellars deep as wounds.
Left behind: The shattered legs, the faces
unnamed, grey or faded blue, decaying
where they fell. I walk the field that sleeps with
its artillery of bones. I dig up
need, sifting through my fingers grain by grain
the loaves that are the fishes. Forgiveness
in my legs, witness in the lips that are
the berry that sustains the sacrament.
Long knives incise the wind's true whisper. They
call me Mother or the name that only
you can call me: Sister, when the sun repeats.

5

Dead Souls
After Chagall

Though we've never met, never wed,
this detail or that I like, you do too.
The sexless circle breasts. The backside of the hero.
We twin as self-appointed critics of the drypoint dinner guests:
The governors, the lords of debt. The piggish boss, the lout.
The madam with the unclean hands commanding traffic court.
We know them as the penciled relatives of haute oppression.
Sketch them in our hate. The War abetted.
Revolution's in the fat of our encephalitic chat.

A Congress of Monsters

A long grey chin reminds you
of Sacco and Vanzetti at a funeral.
You're cynical. Too thin
to costume doubt. Too transparent
in the mask that sometimes answers
squad cars on the block. Sometimes knocks.
Devils in the practices of well-trained cops.
Devils in the lines of conversation.

Voices brew the hunt for witches who undo
the spell of coffee shops. The night is fraught
with treason. Black cats plot anxieties
you thought you'd turned off like the porch light.
The late leaves shiver. Familiars haunt
the sexless breasts at Hooters.
They carve the headless heads
as frost pulls on its glossed Gestapo boots.
The hand that razors apples
seems to know you.

How Light Bends at the Exxon

Behind the bullet glass, he waves, as I wave back.
"Nice day," he says, as if he means the weather.
As if sympathies of heat could teach us better.
Gallons/dollars/cents. Numbers in their lotteries of
cause/effect. $3.99 – no more or less deterrent than
a nuclear solution. The sun is shifting closer.
Pansies in the pot light up like flares. I lift the lever.
Nozzle fitted, air expands. The light reflected
bends. A hundred thousand casualties of
Earth and men. The means like ends. Like shifting
sands under the traffic's caravan. I start the engine.

Sleep of Stones

He bore himself a god in the rumbling that awakened.
A laddered truck at the gate. A berried bower at the fence
where he entered, sent by the landlord to tenant the land
I rented. Ten years I'd tended its wildness. Loved
its toothed margins of leaves. Its thorn.

His mower began its first right:
The daisies spoiled.
The buttercups spilled.
The wise dandelions imploded.
The ivy stripped
of its love of brick
tumbled, rope after rope.

I flamed to it. Fell
out of dream into seasons un-
Edened. Hastened to grief,
I pleaded

for seeds set aloft, for trees.
"The land on which you lie shall be like
dust," he quoted, tasked with his executions.
And behold, he retreated
into summer's gasoline. Into
sleep without dreams. A time of weeping.

Neither Shall You Steal

After shopping at the Big Lots, headed for the car,
she sees the child has something in his fist.
"What's this?" she asks, leaning in.
His small fingers lock around an artificial
flower. A silk gentian from China, so breathtakingly real
she has to feel it when he holds it up, and she says, "Joey,"
the shadow of a frown descending on a child's right from wrong.
She knows she taught him better. "It's for you," he says,
and lifts the flower to her chin, his imitation of a
grown man's love. She slaps his wrist. Insists:
"Take it back," admit your sin to the woman counting
hours at the checkout. His shoulders sink.
He works his sneaker into graveled bits
of her commandments.

Waste of Culture Waste of State

And don't your eyes seek out the things you want?
— Hannibal Lector

A foreplay of signs, designs.
Passion's in the branding: "Got Milk."
Food tastes better cars run faster women look thin.
PVC and cardboard, despite the power strips. Think

global. Like in Rio de Janeiro, art's in landfills.
In the manner of big companies, think
big. Drink
patronage with cereal. Delirium with paint.
Cut off ears for tax breaks.
You get used to the smell.

"I'd walk a mile for a camel," the lung exploding says,
limping into deserts of campaigns
that have changed you
into featureless cities resembling:
A mouth: "Eat Mor." A face across wallscape.
The manufactured feeling seduces.
Woo governors of sinecures. Private fortunes.

It always starts with something true.
Then it isn't. "Where's the beef?"

Food tastes better cars run faster women look thin.
I can make you famous in a week.

Goodnight, Irene

*...what does it matter what reality is outside myself, so long as it has helped me
to live, to feel that I am, and what I am?* — Baudelaire

Neighbors on Sunday swept streets. A nuisance of raking. A car in a
heap, crushed by a tree, up to its wheel wells in water.
A man and his son bagged debris.
We talked on my walk to eyewitness the scene,
and he joked, "What next? Volcanic eruption,"
as bees from felled trees dislocated,

as millions lost power. Elsewhere the trauma downed trees,
the colors advancing, in red yellow green
tracked in the forecast to pass over islands at nightfall,
the eye fall on maps on screens, in brilliant crawlspace.
The landfall in Hatteras, layered: Grey, oyster white, jade green,
roaring toward wreckage in raw, six-foot waves. The rain
inundating. The sea wall
crumbling to rock.

She choked Ocracoke. Cars submerged. Airports locked down.
Ahead of the storm's progression, the federal emergency.
Wind gusts and flooding. Coney Island. Jersey Shore.
Viewers sent pictures and tweets. The boats on their backs.
A history of bridges, tumbling.

We talked of the wind that riffled the trees, clipped branches.
She was "chatty," he said, and I turned back to what I should get:
Batteries, water, canned food. What would I need besides these?
A pen in my hand. A poem in the darkness. Belief.

Once, in a Yellow Wood

The double yellow swam beneath the wake of tractor trailers.
The grey mimicked rain. Headlights wrestled fog.
It was the morning of a very bad decision.

I could say I had it coming. I could say I was unhappy.
A girl with a grudge. An intuition.

The sudden leaves spoke up. They said I'd gone too far to
find the road to take me back.
Oh, foot to the clutch.
Wheels
in the sky. Each
intersecting a wheel.

I rode the rock face 'til I dropped. Slid into the do-si-do of
angels. The grim one on the right was spitting plug.
The other, hobnail clogging.
I was small inside calamities.
                   Collision
when the mountain opened up.

I kicked through the crystal windshield.
A stunt like Houdini's. My shoulder with wing, flighted.
The day mimicked light.
A whiff
before the explosion.

Fear, Desire—Feathers That Fly

The slender fingers of the daffodil
signal their come-hither. The rolling green.
The mountains vaguely blue and beckoning a mythic
distance unperturbed by weather. The screen
is a pretense of landscape: Words, numbers keyed
in reflex realities. A daily feed
of systems that summon me to presence
in the network. Sometimes in a clear and present
mind, I elope into the gardens
where whimsy ferns, where screen gives way
to branches of a pine that stairway
to the blue and clouds departing, sweep aside
the whooing of the thing inside
the thing — downloading.
The air, though chill, sparkles.
Tiger lilies deepen.
So many evergreens agree on shade!
One gnarled, twisting, bonsaied by the canopy
and wind, reminds me what a thing
in nature can become deprived of light,
the mad love of the trees. A bird, death throated, sings.

Ritual of Little Heads

These bulbs like severed heads
sprout consolation. Confession

in the moonlit landscape of the furrowed.
Our blunted hands like roots reach out

to dust. To little gods who think too much.
We think they never love us, rush

to reason when there is no reason
for the dark bird wheeling luck.

Comets trail their ghosts of crust.
We burn out long before the accident of touch,

run from countless stars,
as if we might be crushed.

Blue Moon

In the backyard of my thoughts

             the vast

       and all its definitions had dumbfounded. I bit the hand
that fed imagination, took
for pestilence the flies.

For end of world the gullywashers. I shook
in handfuls petals fetched from

             doubt.

Petals losing memory of pink. The small white cups
that coffin trees. The roses wrought to stem. To thorn.
To weather. The mess of bees. The failed azaleas.

        How was I to know you'd really show?

When I reveled in the lonely, kin to none,
I forgot

the g/loved limbs flinging blossoms at my feet.

          The slippered slug — a soft cigar
       in pistol tincture trailing,
       rolling between blessings and forgetfulness.
       The roof of stars.

What the Body Knows

Cedar Lakes, West Virginia

The cedars preach a magic out there where the rain's an insight.
We are falling — well deep, where none can guess a resurrection.
We remember summer's ghost, the gamble.
The sun's bracelets burning.
The swoon of purple evening.

Someone was here before us.
We see the halo of his footfall in the puddles
as we dance, stumbling backward.

Someone in the current sucks our breath away,
turns darkness on a spindle.

What we don't know
the body tells us. The body knows to make us small.

Diamond Life

Ghost, how well you hide.
I hear your footsteps fleet in dust of time behind
the ochre-colored mound, sometimes giving ground
in rabbits' cunning. You said you didn't see it coming.
Your "third in stolen" stolen. The keys you couldn't find.
The coach who clocked your sprints clocked your disease.

Walk me to release on legs of one great body running.
Desire me the hour of the bee.

Notches

We cut into bone
each winter he lived,

until snow buried everything,
and everything was silent
but the ghost of hunger rising
in our throats.

Dog starved, deer.
Even crow was silent.

Frozen fingers saved from thinning
smoke the last of fire.

We counted moons
until the frost surrendered.
Bear left tracks in thaw.

We buried him with feathers,
the bone
that was the legend of his years.

We danced for ghosts
to take us back
to the beginning,

when but for us
all animals were white as snow.

Smoke

Soundless out of these into the world it goes.
Shape out of nothing, smoke.
Halo or infinity, hoop or a trinity
of rings around the dancer's foot.
Nothing is what seems.
The sky from the horizon is attenuated hope.
A leaf from trees.
A hologram of things begun,
turned back in such degrees
you see it kindle from a rope
of grass. Let it go.
Stoke the pipe and wait until
the lights like boundless fireflies digress.
Flashes through the membrane.

Kathleen Hellen's chapbook *The Girl Who Loved Mothra* (2010)
was published by Finishing Line Press. Her poems have appeared in
numerous journals and were featured on WYPR's *The Signal*. She has
received awards from the Maryland State Arts Council, the Baltimore
Office of Promotion & the Arts, and the Appalachian Writers Associa-
tion, as well as poetry prizes from the *H.O.W Journal*, *Washington Square
Review* and the Thomas Merton prize for Poetry of the Sacred. Born in
Tokyo, Japan, she now lives in Baltimore, Maryland.

About Washington Writers' Publishing House

Washington Writers' Publishing House is a non-profit organization that has published nearly 100 volumes of poetry and fiction since 1975. The press sponsors an annual competition for writers living in the Washington-Baltimore area, and the winners of each category (one each in poetry and fiction) comprise our set of published works each year.

WWPH has received grants from the Lannan Foundation, the National Endowment for the Arts, the DC Commission on the Arts and Humanities, the Nation magazine, and the Poetry Society of America. Many individuals have also assisted, encouraged, and supported our work through the years.

Become a WWPH Author

Submit your book-length poetry or fiction manuscripts to Washington Writers' Publishing House's annual poetry and fiction competitions. Visit our web site at www.washingtonwriters.org for contest guidelines.

Some Recent Titles

Poetry:

Bloodcoal & Honey, by Dan Gutstein
Words We Might One Day Say, by Holly Karapetkova
From the Fever-World, by Jehanne Dubrow
Provenance, by Brandel France de Bravo
Temporary Apprehensions, by Patric Pepper
Gagarin Street, by Piotr Gwiazda

Fiction:

The Color of My Soul, by Melanie S. Hatter
Right of Way, by Andrew Wingfield
Success: Stories, by David A. Taylor
And Silent Left the Place, by Elizabeth Bruce
Nora's Army, by Denis Collins
Can't Remember Playing, by Gretchen Roberts

To order these books or other WWPH titles visit online booksellers like Amazon.com and BarnesandNoble.com, or visit us at www.washingtonwriters.org, or e-mail us at wwphpress@gmail.com.

CPSIA information can be obtained at www.ICGtesting.com
Printed in the USA
BVOW021044060812

297043BV00001B/8/P